RESEARCH LIBRARY
OF
COLONIAL AMERICANA

RESEARCH LIBRARY
OF
COLONIAL AMERICANA

General Editor
RICHARD C. ROBEY
Columbia University

Advisory Editors
JACK P. GREENE
Johns Hopkins University

EDMUND S. MORGAN
Yale University

ALDEN T. VAUGHAN
Columbia University

THE TRUE INTEREST OF BRITAIN, SET FORTH IN REGARD TO THE COLONIES

Jos[iah] Tucker

ARNO PRESS
A New York Times Company
New York – 1972

Reprint Edition 1972 by Arno Press Inc.

Reprinted from a copy in The State Historical
Society of Wisconsin Library

LC# 76-141126
ISBN 0-405-03337-0

Research Library of Colonial Americana
ISBN for complete set: 0-405-03270-6
See last pages of this volume for titles.

Manufactured in the United States of America

Publisher's Note: This volume was reprinted
from the best available copy.

THE TRUE
INTEREST OF BRITAIN,
SET FORTH IN REGARD
TO THE
COLONIES;

And the only MEANS of

Living in PEACE and HARMONY with THEM,

Including Five different Plans, for effecting this desirable Event.

By JOS. TUCKER, D. D. DEAN of GLOCESTER. Author of the Essay on the Advantages and Disadvantages which respectively attend France and Great-Britain, with regard to Trade.

To which is Added by the PRINTER, A few more WORDS, on the FREEDOM of the PRESS in AMERICA.

PHILADELPHIA:
Printed, and Sold, by ROBERT BELL, in Third-Street,
MDCCLXXVI.

THE
True Interest of GREAT-BRITAIN
SET FORTH
In Regard to the COLONIES;
And the only Means of
Living in Peace and Harmony with them:
Including,
Five different Plans
For Effecting this Salutary Measure.

A VERY strange notion is now industriously spreading, that 'till the late unhappy Stamp-Act, there were no bickerings and discontents, no heart-burnings and jealousies subsisting between the Colonies and the Mother-Country. It seems, 'till that fatal period, all was harmony, peace and love. Now it is scarcely possible even for the most superficial observer, if his knowledge extends beyond the limits of a Newspaper, not to know, "that this is entirely false." And if he is at all conversant in the history of the Colonies, and has attended to the accounts of their original Plantation, their rise and progress, he

A 'must

must know, that almost from the very beginning, there were mutual discontents, mutual animosities and reproaches. Indeed, while these Colonies were in a mere state of infancy, dependent on their Mother-Country not only for daily protection, but almost for daily bread, it cannot be supposed that they would give themselves the same airs of self-sufficiency and independence, as they did afterwards, in proportion as they grew up to a state of maturity. But that they began very early to shew no other marks of attachment to their ancient parent, than what arose from views of self-interest and self-love, many convincing proofs might be drawn from the complaints of, and the instructions to the Governors of the respective Provinces; from the memorials of our Boards of Trade, presented from time to time to his Majesty's Privy Council against the behaviour of the Colonists; from the frequent petitions and remonstrances of our Merchants and Manufacturers to the same effect; and even from the votes and resolutions of several of their Provincial Assemblies against the interest, laws, and Government of the Mother-Country; yet I will wave all these at present, and content myself with proofs still more authentic and unexceptionable; I mean the public Statutes of the Realm: For from them it evidently appears, that long before there were any thoughts of the Stamp-Act, the Mother-Country had the following accusations to bring against the Colonies, viz. 1st, that they refused to submit to her

her ordinances and regulations in regard to Trade.—2dly, that they attempted to frame Laws, and to erect Jurisdiction not on y independently of her, but even in direct opposition to her authority.—And 3dly, that many of them took unlawful methods to skreen themselves from paying the just debts they owed to the Merchants and Manufacturers of Great-Britain.

These are the objections of the Mother-Country to the behaviour of the colonies long before their last outrages, and their present conduct:—For even as early as the year 1670, it doth appear, that MANY COMPLAINTS (the very words of the Act) had been made against the AMERICAN Proprietors of Ships and Vessels, for engaging in Schemes of Traffic, contrary to the regulations contained in the act of Navigation, and in other statutes of the Realm made for confining the trade of the Colonies to the Mother-Country. Nay, so sensible was the Parliament above an hundred Years ago, that Prosecutions for the breach of those laws would be to little or no effect, if carried on in AMERICAN Courts, or before AMERICAN Juries, that it is expressly ordained, " It shall, it may be law-
" ful for any person or persons to prosecute
" such Ship or Vessel [offending as described in
" the preceding Section] in any Court of Ad-
" miralty in England; the one moiety of the
" forfeiture, in case of condemnation, to be
" to his Majesty, his Heirs, and successors; and
" the other Moiety to such Prosecutor or
" Prosecutors thereof." See 22 and 23 of Ch.
II.

II. Cap. 26. § 12 and 13.] And we find, that two years afterwards, viz. 25 of Ch. II. Cap. 7, the same complaints were again renewed; and in consequence thereof higher duties and additional penalties were laid on, for the more effectually enforcing of the observance of this and of the former laws: But in spite of all that was done, things grew worse and worse every day. For it is observable, that in the year 1696, the very authority of the English Legislature, for making such laws and regulations, seemed to have been called in question; which authority, therefore, the Parliament was obliged to assert in terms very peremptory;---- and I may likewise add, very prophetical. The Law made on this occasion was the famous Statute of the 7th and 8th of William III. Cap. 7. wherein, after the recital of divers acts " made for the encouragement of the Naviga- " tion of this Kingdom, and for the better se- " curing and regulating the Plantation Trade, " it is remarked, that notwithstanding such laws, " great abuses are daily committed, to the pre- " judice of the English Navigation, and the " Loss of great part of the Plantation trade " to this Kingdom, by the artifice and cunning " of ill-disposed Persons." Then, having prescribed such remedies as these great evils seemed to require, the Act goes on at §. 7. to ordain, " That all the penalties and Forfeitures " before mentioned, not in this act particu- " larly disposed of, shall be one third part to " the use of his Majesty, his Heirs, and Suc-
" cessors,

"cessors, and one third part to the Governor
"of the Colony or Plantation where the offence
"shall be committed, and the other third part
"to such person or persons as shall sue for the
"same, to be recovered in any of his majesty's
"courts at Westminster, or in the kingdom of
"Ireland, or in the courts of Admiralty held in
"his majesty's Plantations respectively, where
"such offence shall be committed, "at the plea-
"sure of the Officer or Informer, or in any other
"Plantation belonging to any subject of England
"wherein no Essoin, protection, or wager of
"Law shall be allowed; and that where any
"question shall arise concerning the importa-
"tion or exportation of any goods into or out
"of the said plantations, in such case the proof
"shall lie upon the owner or claimer; and the
"claimer shall be reputed to be the importer or
"owner thereof."

Now here it is obvious to every reader, that the suspicions which the Parliament had formerly conceived of the partiality of American Courts, and American Juries in trials at Law with the Mother-Country, were so far from being abated by length of time, that they were grown higher than ever; because it appears by this very act, that the power of the Officer or Informer was greatly enlarged, having the option now granted him of three different Countries for prosecuting the offence; whereas in the former of Charles II. made 16 years before, he had only two. Moreover it was this time further ordained, that the Onus
probandi

probandi should rest on the defendant, and also that no * Essoin, Protection. or † Wager of law should be allowed him.

But above all, and in order to prevent, if possible every sort of chicane for the future, and to frustrate all attempts of the Colonies, either to throw off or evade the power and jurisdiction of the Mother-Country,—It was at § 9. " further enacted and declared by the au-
" thority aforesaid, that all Laws, Bye Laws,
" Usages, or Customs, at this time, or which
" hereafter shall be in practice, or endeavoured,
" or pretended to be in force or practice, in any
" of the said Plantations, which are in any wise
" repugnant to the before mentioned Laws, or
" any of them, so far as they do relate to the
" said Plantations, or any of them, or which are
" any ways repugnant to this present Act, or
" to any other law hereafter to be made in
" this KINGDOM, so far as such Law shall re-
" late to, and mention the said Plantations, are
" ILLEGAL, Null, and Void to all INTENTS
" and PURPOSES Whatsoever."

Words could be hardly devised to express the sentiments of the English Legislature, more fully and strongly, than these have done: And if ever a body of uninspired Men were endowed with

---

* An Essoin signifies, in Law, a pretence or excuse.
† A Wager at Law, is a power granted to the Defendant to swear, together with other COMPURGATORS, that he owes nothing to the Plaintiff in the manner set forth.——It is easy to see what use would have been made of such a power had it been allowed.

with a spirit of Divination, or of foreseeing, and also of providing against untoward future events, as far as human prudence could extend, the King, Lords, and Commons of the Æra 1696, were the very Men. For they evidently foresaw, that a time was approaching, when the Provincial assemblies would dispute the Right of AMERICAN Sovereignty with the great and general Council of the BRITISH Empire: And therefore they took effectual care that, whenever the time came, no law, no precedent, nor prescription, should be wanting, whereby the Mother-Country might assert her constitutional and inherent right over the Colonies.

But notwithstanding these wise Precautions, some of the Colonies found ways and means to evade the Force and meaning even of this express law; at least for a time, and 'till the Legislature could be sufficiently apprized of the injury designed. The Colonists, who practised these disingenuous arts with most success, were those who were endowed with chartered Governments, and who in consequence of the extraordinary favours thereby indulged them, could nominate or elect their own Council, and (if my memory doth not fail me) their own Governors likewise;—at least, who could grant such salaries to their Governors, and with such limitations, as would render them too dependent on the will and pleasure of their Pay-Masters. Hence therefore it came to pass, that in the Colonies of Rhode-Island and Providence Plantations, Connecticut, the Massachuset's Bay,

and

and New Hampfhire; the Governors of thefe Provinces fuffered themfelves to be perfuaded to give their fanction to certain Votes and Refolutions of their Affemblies and Councils; whereby laws were enacted firft to iffue out bills of Credit to a certain amount, and then to make a tender of thofe bills to be confidered as an adequate difcharge of debts, and a legal releafe from payment. A moft compendious method this for getting out of debt! And were the like artifice to be authorized every where, I think it is very evident, that none but the moft ftupid Ideot would be incapable of difcharging his debts, bonds, or obligations; and that too without advancing any money.

However, as foon as the Britifh Legiflature came to be fully apprifed of this fcheme of iniquity, they paffed a Law, " to regulate and " reftrain paper Bills of Credit in his Majefty's " Colonies or Plantations, of Rhode Ifland and " Providence Plantations, Connecticut, the Maf- " fachufets Bay, and New Hampfhire in Ame- " rica; and to prevent the fame being le- " gal tenders in payments of money."——— This is the very title of the Statute; but for further particulars, and for the different regulations therein contained, confult the act itfelf, 24th of George II. Cap. 53, Anno 1751.

Now will any Man after this dare to fay, that the Stamp-Act was the firft caufe of diffention betwen the Mother-Country and her Colonies? Will any Man ftill perfift in maintaining fo grofs a Paradox, that 'till that fatal period, the Colonies

lonies shewed no reluctance to submit to the commercial regulations, no disposition to contest the authority, and no desire to question the right of the Mother-Country? The man who can maintain these paradoxes, is incapable of conviction, and therefore is not to be reasoned with any longer. " But the Stamp-Act " made bad to become worse :———The Stamp- " Act irritated and inflamed, and greatly en- " creased all those ill humours, which were but " too predominant before." Granted; and I will further add, that any other act, or any other measure, of the British Government, as well as the Stamp-Act, if it were to compel the Colonists to contribute a single shilling towards the general expence of the British Empire, would have had the same effect. For, be it ever remembered, that the Colonists did not so much object to the mode of this taxation, as to the right itself of levying taxes. Nay, their friends and agents here in England were known to have frequently declared, that if any tax were to be crammed down their throats without their consent, and by an authority which they disallowed, they had rather pay this Stamp-Duty than another.

But indeed, and properly speaking, it was not the Stamp-Act which increased or heightened these ill humours in the Colonists; rather, it was the reduction of Canada, which called forth those dispositions into action which had long been generating before; and which were ready to burst forth at the first opportunity that should offer. For an undoubted fact it is, that from the moment in which Canada came into the possession of the English, an end was put to the Sovereignty of the Mother-Country over her Colonies. They had then nothing to fear from a foreign enemy; and as to their own domestic friends and relations, they had for so many years preceding been accustomed to trespass upon their forbearance and indulgence, even when they most wanted their protection, that it was no wonder they should openly renounce an authority which they never thorougly approved of, and which now they found to be no longer necessary for their own defence.

But here some may be apt to ask, " Had the " Colonies no provocation on their part? And " was all the fault on one side, and none on " the other ?" Probably not :—probably there were faults on both sides. But what doth this serve to prove? If to exculpate the Colonies in regard to their present refractory behaviour, it is needless. For I am far from charging our Colonies in particular with being sinners above others; because I believe (and If I am wrong, let the history of all Colonies, whether ancient or modern, from the days of THUCYDIDES down to the present time, confute me if it can; I say, till that is done I believe) that it is the nature of them all to aspire after Independence, and to set up for themselves as soon as ever they find that they are able to subsist, without being beholden to the Mother-Country. And if our
Americans

Americans have expressed themselves sooner on this head than others have done, or in a more direct and daring manner, this ought not to be imputed to any greater malignity, or ingratitude in them, than in others, but to that bold free constitution, which is the prerogative and boast of us all. We ourselves derive our origin from those very SAXONS; who inhabited the lower parts of Germany; and yet I think it is sufficiently evident, that we are not over complaisant to the descendants of these lower SAXONS, i. e. to the offspring of our own Progenitors; nor can we, with any colour of reason, pretend to complain that even the Bostonians have treated us more indignantly than we have treated the Hanoverians. What then would have been the case, if the little insignificant Electorate of Hanover had presumed to retain a claim of Sovereignty over such a Country as Great-Britain, the pride and Mistress of the Ocean? And yet, I believe, that in point of extent of Territory, the present Electoral Dominions, insignificant as they are sometimes represented, are more than a moiety of England, exclusive of Scotland and Wales: whereas the whole Island of Great Britain, is scarcely a twentieth part of those vast Regions which go under the denomination of North-America.

Besides, if the American Colonies belonging to France or Spain, have not yet set up for Independence, or thrown off the masque so much as the English Colonies have done,--what is this superior reserve to be imputed to? Not to any greater filial tenderness in them for their respective antient Parents than in others ;---not to motives of any national gratitude, or of national honour;---but because the constitution of each of those Parent States is much more arbitrary and despotic than the constitution of Great-Britain; and therefore their respective offsprings are * awed by the dread of punishments from breaking forth into those outrages which ours dare do with impunity. Nay more, the very Colonies of France and Spain, though they have not yet thrown off their allegiance, are nevertheless as forward as any in disobeying the Laws of their Mother-Countries, wherever they find an interest in so doing. For the truth of this fact, I appeal to that prodigious clandestine Trade which they are continually carrying on with us, and with our Colonies, contrary to the express prohibitions of France and Spain: And I appeal also to those very free ports which the British Legislature itself hath lately opened for accommodating these smuggling colonists to trade with the subjects of Great-Britain, in Disobedience to the injunction of their Mother-Countries.

Enough surely has been said on this subject; and the upshot of the whole matter is plainly this,---

---

* But notwithstanding this awe, it is now pretty generally known, that the French Colonists of Hispaniola endeavoured lately to shake off the Government of Old France, and applied to the British Court for that purpose.

this,---That even the arbitrary and despotic Governments of France and Spain (arbitrary I say, both in temporals and in spirituals) maintain their authority over their American Colonies but very imperfectly; in as much as they cannot restrain them from breaking through those rules and regulations of exclusive trade; for the sake of which all Colonies seemed to have been originally founded. What then shall we say in regard to such Colonies as are the offspring of a free constitution? And after what manner, or according to what rule, are our own in particular to be governed, without using any force or compulsion, or pursuing any measure repugnant to their own ideas of civil or religious Liberty? In short, and to sum up all, in one word, how shall we be able to render these Colonies more subservient to the interests, and more obedient to the laws and government of the Mother-Country, than they voluntarily chuse to be? After having pondered and revolved the affair over and over, I confess, there seems to me to be but the five following proposals, which can possibly be made, viz.

1st, To suffer things to go on for a while, as they have lately done, in hopes that some favourable opportunity may offer for recovering the jurisdiction of the BRITISH Legislature over her Colonies, and for maintaining the authority of the Mother-Country.---Or if these temporising measures should be found to strengthen and confirm the evil, instead of removing it;---then,

2dly,

2dly, To attempt to perſwade the Colonies to ſend over a certain number of Deputies, or Repreſentatives, to ſit and vote in the BRITISH parliament; in order to incorporate AMERICA and GREAT BRITAIN into one common Empire,---Or if this Propoſal ſhould be found impracticable, whether on account of the Difficulties attending it on this ſide of the Atlantic, or becauſe that the Americans themſelves would not concur in ſuch a meaſure; then,

3dly, To declare open War againſt them as Rebels and Revolters; and after having made a perfect Conqueſt of the Country, then to govern it by Military Force and deſpotic ſway.---Or if this ſcheme ſhould be judged (as it ought to be) the moſt deſtructive, and the leaſt eligible of any;---then,

4thly, To propoſe to conſent that AMERICA ſhould become the General Seat of Empire; and that Great Britain and Ireland ſhould be governed by Vice-Roys ſent over from the Court Reſidencies, either at Philadelphia or New-York, or at ſome other American imperial City,----Or if this plan of Accommodation ſhould be ill-digeſted by home-born Engliſhmen, who, I will venture to affirm, would never ſubmit to ſuch an Indignity;---then,

5thly, To propoſe to ſeparate entirely from the Colonies, by declaring them to be a free and Independent People, over whom we lay no Claim; and then by offering to guarantee this Freedom and Independence againſt all foreign Invaders whomſoever.

Now

Now these being all the plans which, in the nature of things, seem capable of being proposed, let us examine each of them in their order.

FIRST PLAN.

And 1st, as to that which recommends the suffering all things to go on as they have lately done, in hopes that some favourable opportunity may arise hereafter for recovering the jurisdiction, and vindicating the honour of the Mother-Country.

This first proposal is very unhappy at first setting out; because it takes that for granted, which history and experience prove to be false. It supposes, that Colonies may become the more obedient, in proportion as they are suffered to grow the more headstrong, and to feel their own strength and independence; than which supposition there cannot be a more palpable absurdity. For if a father is not able to govern his son at the ages of 14 or 16 years, how can it be supposed that he will be better able when the youth is become a man of full age and stature, in the vigour of health and strength, and the parent perhaps more feeble and decrepid than he was before? Besides, it is a fact, that the Colonies, from almost one end of North-America to the other, have already revolted from under the jurisdiction of the British Legislature;—each House of Assembly hath already arrogated to themselves a new name, by stiling themselves an HOUSE OF COMMONS; in consequence of which stile and title, they have
already

already declared, that the British House of Commons neither hath, nor ought to have, any right to intermeddle in their concerns. Now, after they have advanced thus far already, what Rhetoric would you use for calling these revolters back? And is it at all probable, that the Provincial Assemblies would be induced by the force of oratory to renounce their own importance, and to acknowledge that to be a crime, which both they, and the people whom they represent, glory as in their birth-right and unalienable prerogative? The man who can suppose these things, must have a most extraordinary opinion of his own eloquence.

But here perhaps some may be inclined to ask, Why would you meddle with the Colonies at all? And why not suffer things to remain in statu quo? The obvious answer to which questions is this,—That it is not the Mother Country which meddles with the Colonies, but the Colonies which meddle with the Mother-Country: For they will not permit her to govern in the manner she ought to do, and according to the original terms of the constitution; but are making encroachments on her authority every day. Moreover as they increase in riches, strength, and numbers, their civil and military establishments must necessarily increase likewise; and seeing that this circumstance is unavoidable, who is to defray the growing expences of these increasing and thriving Colonies? " The Colonies themselves
" you will naturally say, because none are so fit,
" and

" and none so able :" And perhaps some American advocates will likewise add, " That the
" Colonies do not refuse to defray these expences, provided they shall be the sole judges
" of the quantum to be raised, or the mode of
" raising it, and of the manner of its application." But here lies the difficulty, which remains yet to be solved: For if the Colonies are to be allowed to be the sole judges in these matters, the sovereignty of the British Legislature is entirely at an end; and these Colonies become in fact, as much independent of their Mother-Country, as we are independent of Hanover, or Hanover of us;—only indeed with this difference (which an American always chuses to forget) That whereas we lay a duty on all raw materials coming from the Electoral Dominions, we give a bounty on those which are imported from the Colonies. Besides, many will be apt to ask, could not this matter be compromised in some degree? And will nothing less content the Colonies than a total revolt from under the jurisdiction of the Mother-Country?——Some well-meaning persons have proposed, that each Colony, like each County here in England, should be allowed to raise taxes for its own internal uses, whilst the British parliament, the sovereign council of the British Empire, should preside over the whole; and therefore should enact such laws for the levying of those general taxes, which are to be applied for the common protection, the good, and benefit

of all. But the misfortune is, that the Colonies will not consent to this partition of power and jurisdiction; consequently any scheme of this nature is utterly impracticable. Indeed the late Stamp-Act itself was no other than a part of this very scheme: For the money to be raised by that tax, was to be applied to the sole use of the Colonies, and to be expended no where else but in the Colonies. Nay it was not the moiety, nor yet the third, nor the fourth part of the sum which Great-Britain was to have raised on the same account, and to have expended in the same Provinces:—So anxious was the antient indulgent parent not to lay too heavy a burden on her favourite children. But alas! Favourites of all kinds seldom make those returns of gratitude and obedience, which might be expected. For even as to that boasted loyalty, which the colonies have hitherto professed to maintain towards his Majesty King George,—this stands, and must stand, according to their present political system, on as precarious a footing as any of the rest of our claims. For if the British parliaments have no right to make laws to bind the Colonies, they certainly ought not to be allowed to prescribe to them " who shall be their King;—much less ought they to pretend to a right of enacting, That it shall be a most capital offence, even " high treason" itself, in a colonist to dare to controvert the title of any prince, or any family, to the American throne, whom the British Parliament shall place thereon.

BESIDES,

BESIDES, some of those lower Houses of Assemblies (which each Province now affects to call its House of Commons) have already proceeded to greater lengths of sovereignty and independence than a British House of Commons ever presumed to do except in the days of the grand rebellion. For they have already arrogated to themselves a power of disposing, as well as of raising the public monies, without the consent of the other branches of the legislature; which is, in fact, nothing less than the erection of so many sovereign and independent Democracies. Nay more, there is a general combination and confederacy entered into among them all: For each House of Assembly hath lately appointed a standing committee for corresponding with the standing committees of other Provinces, in order the more effectually to oppose the authority and jurisdiction of the Mother-Country.

WHAT then is to be done in such a case? Evident it is beyond a dispute, that timid and temporising measures serve to no other purpose but that of confirming the colonies in their opposition, and strengthening them in their present revolt.

PLAN Second.

WHEREFORE the 2d proposal is, To attempt to persuade the Colonies to send over a certain number of Representatives to sit and vote in the BRITISH Parliaments, in order to incorporate AMERICA and GREAT-BRITAIN into one common Empire.

* This

* This is the scheme of a very worthy gentleman, eminently versed in the laws and constitution of Great-Britain, and what is still better, a real, not a pretended Patriot. Let us therefore examine it with as much respect and deference to his opinion, as the cause of truth will permit; which I am well persuaded, is full as much as he would require.

He begins with observing very justly, page 4. "That the subjects of the Crown of Great-Britain, must (i. e. ought to) continue to be so in every respect, in all parts of the world, where they live under the protection of the British Government; and that their crossing the Atlantic Ocean with the King's licence, and residing in America for the purposes of trade, cannot affect their legal subjection to the governing powers of the community to which they belong.

"But yet he observes, that the total want of Representatives in the great Council of the nation, to support their interests, and give an assent on their behalf to laws and taxes by which they are bound and affected, is a misfortune, which every friend to liberty and equal government must be sorry to see them labour under, and from which he must wish them to be relieved in a regular and constitutional "manner,

---

* See a Pamphlet,——" Considerations on the Expediency of admitting Representatives from the AMERICAN Colonies into the British House of Commons."——LONDON, printed for B. WHITE, 1770.

"manner, if such relief can possibly be af-
"forded them, without breaking the unity of
"the British Government."

He therefore proceeds, at page 10, to propose his scheme for remedying this misfortune; viz "That about eighty persons might be ad-
"mitted to sit in Parliament, as members of
"the Commons House of Parliament for all the
"Kings's Dominions in America, the West-
"Indies, as well as North America; and that
"their Stile and Title should be " The Com-
"missioners of the Colonies of AMERICA."
After this he goes on to fix the numbers requisite to represent each Colony, their qualification, and the mode of their election; also the time of their continuing in office, and the manner of their being re-elected, or superseded by others, if that should be judged necessary: In all which, tho' the proposals are not quite consistent with the unity of the British Government, yet as he has obviated the principal difficulties, it would be both ill-natured and unjust to spy out every small fault, or to magnify objections.

But when he comes to give us the form, the Extent and the limitation of these Commissions; nay, when he proposes to circumscribe the authority and jurisdiction of the British Parliament itself, even after it hath been strengthened by the accession of these Colony-Representatives; there, I humbly apprehend, the importance of the subject should preponderate over mere deference and complaisance.

Nay

Nay I will go still further, and add, that if the measures proposed should be shewn to have a tendency to beget endless jealousies, quarrels, and divisions, between the Mother-Country and the Colonies, instead of proving a means of reconciliation, and a center of union, the Gentleman himself, I am fully persuaded, would be among the first in rejecting his own plan. Let us therefore now descend into particulars.

And 1st, it is proposed, page 11, that they (the commissioners) should receive a commission in writing from their Electors, viz. (the * Assemblies in each Province) " impowering " them to sit and vote in the British House of " Commons, and consult with the King, and " the Great Men of the Kingdom, and the " Commons of the same in Parliament assem- " bled, upon the great affairs of the Nation, and " to CONSENT on the behalf of the Province, " for which they were chosen, to such things as " shall be ordained in Parliament, &c.

Now this Form might pass very well among ourselves at Home, where the majority are not continually on the watch to spy out every flaw, real or imaginary: But in regard to the Colonists,

---

* QUERE, Whether it is intended that the Lower Houses in each Assembly should have the sole Right of voting for these Commissioners? Or both Houses jointly? If the former, then the Colony Governments would become still more democratical than they now are, tho' already so, to such an excessive degree, as to be almost incompatible with an idea of Monarchy, but if each House is to vote separately, what jars and factions, and reciprocal reproaches, would this occasion! And how would they be able to agree? In short, either way, the prospect is alarming!

nists, and especially an Assembly of Colonists, the case is widely different; For it is well known that their wits are perpetually at work to avail themselves even of the shadow of an Argument to oppose the Right and Authority of the Mother-country. Therefore they will immediately seize on the words impowering and consent, and reason after the following fallacious manner:---" The Assemblies who elected the
" Commissioners, have a Right to instruct
" them; and these Instructions, when properly
" drawn up, are no other than so many trusts
" or powers granted to them from Time to
" time, by the assembly which elected them;
" which Assembly hath therefore a Right to
" contract or enlarge their Commission, as they
" shall find it to be the Interest of the Province
" so to do. Consequently, if these Commis-
" sioners should at any Time Vote contrary to
" their instructions, that is, to their commission,
" it follows, that in these respects they have
" exceeded the bounds prescribed by their Elec-
" tors. Therefore, being themselves prohibi-
" ted from voting, and having no authority to
" vote in such a Question, every Law wherein
" they gave their suffrage, affecting the Interests
" of the Colonies in general, or any province
" in particular, is Ipso Facto Null and Void."
Again.---" The Colony Commissioners are
" to give their consent in behalf of the Province
" for which they are chosen, to such things as
" shall be ordained in Parliament. This is the
" Foundation and Corner-Stone of all the Build-
" ing

" ing: and therefore, if such commissioners
" did not give their consent in behalf of the
" Provinces for which they were chosen, then
" it follows, of course that no law, affecting
" the interests of such respective Provinces, is
" obligatory, no tax due or payable, nor any
" regulations made by the pretended authority
" of the British Parliament without the con-
" sent of such commissioners, are to be at all
" regarded by the American Electors."---These
are a few of those blessed conclusions, which
the Politicians on the other side of the Atlantic
will certainly draw from the terms and expres-
sions contained in such a form. And what is
still worse, both our own hair-brained Repub-
licans, and our Mock Patriots at Home will as
certainly adopt the same language, and echo
back the same specious, tho' false allegations,
from one end of the Kingdom to the other.
Indeed many there are, even among ourselves,
who with the most honest and upright inten-
tions, are at a loss at present how to disintangle
themselves from these fallacious reasonings.
For having unhappily learnt in Newspaper Dis-
sertations, and from coffee-house harangues,
that the Deputies sent to the great Council of
the Nation, are the mere Attornies of those who
elected them; ---the inference is but natural,
that these Attornies ought to do as they are bid;
and that in case of competition, they ought
not to prefer their own private opinions to the
judgments of their constituents.--- I say, this
inference is natural; nay it is necessary, just,

and

and true, were the premises but true from whence it is deduced.

Wherefore, having often had the advantage of hearing no less a person than the late excellent Judge Foster, that true friend to all reasonable liberty, civil and religious,— I say, having often heard him discoursing on the rise and origin of parliaments, I will venture to lay his state of the case before my reader, hoping that it may remove all his difficulties (if he has any) and work the same fullness of conviction in his mind, which it did in mine.

"To reason accurately, said this upright and able lawyer, on the origin of Parliaments, we must trace the matter up to its constituent principles. Now the first idea which strikes one on this occasion is, that of a large Assembly of different tribes of warriors, either preparing for some military expedition, or got together, after a victory, to share the booty and divide the lands among the conquerors. When all are met together in one place, they chuse a Committee for managing their affairs; having found it impracticable to transact any business of consequence in any other way. Now this Committee, chosen by the whole Nation, actually assembled, gives us the first rude draught of a National Parliament, or a National Council. But in process of time, and when the Nation had made large conquests, and was cantoned into distant provinces, it was found to be extremely "inconvenient

"inconvenient to assemble the whole Nation to-
"together into one place. Therefore the next,
"and indeed the only expedient, was, that each
"canton or each district, which could assemble
"should be authorised to elect a deputy, or
"deputies, "not for itself alone, that is the
"grand mistake" but for the Nation at large
"which could not assemble; and the powers
"to be granted to such deputy or deputies, were
"just the same as the nation would have grant-
"ed to them, had it been actually assembled.
"Hence therefore it comes to pass, that each
"deputy represents the whole Nation in gene-
"ral, as much as if he had been elected by the
"whole Nation; and consequently such a de-
"puty is the Attorney, (if he must be called by
"by that name) not of any one particular
"Tribe, Society or District, but of the whole
"collectively: So that it becomes the duty of
"his office to take care of the interests of all
"the people in general, because he represents
"them all. In short, he cannot consistently
"with the duty which he owes to the whole
"pay any deference to the request, instruction,
"remonstrance, or memorial, of his particular
"electors, except in such cases only wherein he
"is convinced in his conscience, that the mea-
"sures, which they require him to pursue, are
"not incompatible with the public good."

Thus far this great Judge of the British constitution. And tho' many important inferences
might be drawn from hence, which would effectually remove those difficulties, with which
the

the Subject has of late been artfully and studiously perplexed (and particularly in the case of the expulsion * of a Member of the House of Commons) yet I shall content myself with one general remark at present; viz. That as each class of Men, each Society or District, throughout the British Empire, are as much represented by those deputies, whom they did not personally elect, as they are by those whom they did; it therefore follows, that there is no need, that the deputies, particularly elected by them, should give their personal consent to any acts of the Legislature; because a vote of the majority is in fact a vote of the Nation to all intents and purposes.

But it is now high time to atttend to another part of this Gentleman's plan for admitting Commissioners from the Colonies to sit and vote in the British House of Commons.

And that is, 2dly the extent of their commission, and indeed the boundary line prescribed to the British Parliament itself, whenever it shall interfere in American affairs. For it seems (see p. 14.) " That this legislative power of Parlia-
" ment should be exercised but seldom, and on
" occasions of great necessity. Whatever re-
" lated

---

* Surely the Nation might have expelled Mr. Wilkes, or have struck his name out of the list of Committee, had it been assembled, and had it thought proper so to do. What then should hinder the Deputies of the Nation from doing the same thing? And which ought to prevail in this case, the Nation in general, or the County of MIDDLESEX?

"lated to the internal government of any particular Colony (such as raising the necessary taxes for the support of its civil government, passing laws for building bridges, or Churches, or Barracks, or other public Edifices) should be left to the Governor and Assembly of that Colony to transact among themselves, unless in cases where the domestic dissentions of the Colony put a stop to public business, and created a kind of necessity for the interposition of the supreme Legislature. But when any general Tax was to be imposed upon all the American Colonies for the support of a war, or any other such general purpose; or any new law was to be made to regulate the Trade of all the Colonies; or to appoint the methods by which debts owing from the Inhabitants of one Colony to those of another, or of Great-Britain, should be recovered; or to direct the manner of bringing Criminals to justice who have fled from one Colony to another; or to settle the manner of quartering the King's Troops in the several Colonies; or of levying Troops in them, and the number each Colony should contribute; or to settle the proportionable values of different coins that should be made current in the several Provinces; or to establish a general Paper-Currency throughout America; or for any other general purpose that relates to several Colonies:—In these cases the authority of Parliament should be employed."

Here now is a kind of barrier set up between

tween these two contending powers, the British Parliament, and the Provincial Assemblies;—a barrier, which must be held so sacred by both parties, as to limit their respective pretensions, and to extinguish all further claims. Let us therefore see how well this scheme is calculated to answer to such good purposes.

And first it is said, that the Parliament ought to interfere but seldom; and then only on occasions of great necessity. Now here permit me to ask, who are to be the Judges of what is seldom, or what is frequent? Moreover, who is to determine between the Parliament and the Provincial Assemblies, when there is a great necessity for the interference of the former, and when there is but a litle one, or none at all?— Obvious it is, to all the World, that these jealous rivals will never settle such points among themselves; and if they will not settle them, indeed if they cannot, who is to be their commmon Umpire or Referee? Besides, granting even that this difficulty could be got over in some degree, another formidable one immediately starts up like another Hydra; viz. What are these Colony-Agents to do in our House of Commons, when no Colony-business happens to be transacted? Are they to remain as so many MUTES, without speaking a word, or giving a single vote for weeks, or months, or perhaps for a whole session together?—Or are they to sit and vote in all British causes, great or small; notwithstanding that the British Senators are precluded from voting, excepting in

extraordinary

extraordinary cases, in respect to the Colonies; In either case here seems to be something introduced into the British constitution of a very heterogeneous nature; something very repugnant to that unity of government, which the Gentleman himself allows ought to be preferred to every other consideration: And I will add further, that if the Colony Commissioners are to sit and vote in all our causes, tho' our British Representatives are restrained from voting in theirs, perhaps ninety-nine times in an hundred, this will be the setting up of one of the most partial, unequal, and unjust systems of pacifications, that ever yet appeared in the World.

We therefore proceed to another weighty objection against the present plan.—The terms of this new compact are declared to be, that the Colony Assemblies shall be invested with the right of internal and Provincial jurisdiction and Legislation; while the British Parliament, even after the Accession of these 80 Colony Commissioners, shall be content to retain only that which is external and general.———But here alas! the very same difficulties return which pressed so hard before: For who is to judge between the British parliament and the Provincial Assemblies in these respects? Who will venture to ascertain in every case what is external and general; and what is merely internal and provincial? Nay indeed, may not the very same things justly pass under both denominations, according as they are seen from different

points

points of view? Surely they may; and to convince any man of this, let him attend to the very catalogue of articles, with which this Gentleman hath himself presented us. For at page 14, he observes, " That whatever related " to the internal governnent, of any particular " Colony, should be left to the Governor and " Assembly of that Colony to transact among " themselves;" among which articles belonging to internal government he enumerates the building of Barracks, and of other Public Edifices; and yet both he and every man must allow, that the building of Barracks, of Forts and Fortresses, the making of King's Docks and careening places for the Navy, the laying out of military roads, and the providing of magazines for provisions and military stores, considered in another view, are of a general nature; in the erection and preservation of which, the whole British Empire is deeply interested. And yet were the British Parliament to frame laws, and to levy taxes on the AMERICANS for these purposes, what outcries would immediately be raised against the Mother-Country! Every Fortress, nay every Barrack, would be described as an odious badge of slavery; and every little Magazine would be termed a monumennt of tyranny and despotic power, and a prerogative for destroying the few liberties that were left. Again, at the bottom of the same Page, he declares, that the authority of Parliament should be employed in settling the manner of quartering the King's troops in the several Colonies.

nies. I will not object to the interposition of Parliament in such a case: For I well know, that if the Parliament did not interfere, the troops would very often have no quarters at all; and yet this very circumstance would afford an AMERICAN Assembly the most inviting opportunity for exclamation and opposition. "What! "the British Parliament to take upon them the "manner of quartering troops in our own "Province, and on our own Inhabitants! who "so proper Judges as ourselves, when or where, "or after what manner, they should be quar- "tered? And how came the Gentlemen, met "at WESTMINSTER, to be acquainted with the "circumstances of our People, and the situation "of places, better than we who reside on the "spot? No! These acts of the BRITISH Par- "liament are all barefaced encroachments on "our liberties, and open violations of our "Rights and Properties: they are the chains "which our pretended protectors, but in reality "our EGYPTIAN task-masters, have been long "forging for us. Let therefore all unite and "manfully resist them; let us postpone the pay- "ing of debts, and enter into a general associati- "on to refuse their goods, to distress their trade, "and to harrass our cruel enemies by every me- "thod in our power; and if we are thus "united, they must yield, as they did before." In short it would be endless to recount all the topics which such a scheme as this Gentleman has proposed, would certainly furnish to every popular Declaimer in every popular Assembly;

and

and the more improbable, the more abſurd and unjuſt his harangues were in point of ſound argument and juſt reaſoning; ſo much generally ſpeaking, the more greedily would they be received.

However, there is one point more which I cannot omit, becauſe it will throw a further light on this matter, and diſcloſe a new ſcene of patriotic manœuvres, and the wiles of Politicians: at page 13, this author lays down a general rule for the conduct of parliament with reſpect to America, " That it ought " to be made a ſtanding order of both Houſes " of Parliament, never to paſs any law, whe- " ther for impoſing a tax, or for regulating " trade, or for any other purpoſe whatſoever " relating to any of the American Colonies, 'till " one whole year after the firſt reading of the " bill; unleſs it be to renew ſome expiring " laws of great importance, and of immediate " and urgent neceſſity, ſuch as the act for " billeting the King's Troops, and perhaps " ſome few others that might be ſpecially excepted in the order."

This is the reſtriction in point of time, which our author propoſes to lay on the Parliament of Great-Britain. " They never muſt " paſs any law for impoſing a tax 'till one " whole year after the firſt reading of the bill:" Why?—In order to give the ſeveral Colonies " an opportunity of making proper repreſenta- " tions againſt it, and to prevent the Parliament "from making injudicious laws, not suited to the condition of the Colonies." A fine contrivance truly! and a most effectual expedient to prevent the Parliament from ever making any laws to oblige the Americans to discharge their duty towards their Mother-Country: For this Gentleman might have known, indeed it is hardly possible, that the fact could have escaped his notice, had he recollected it, that this very circumstance of a year's procrastination was the main engine employed to batter down the late stamp-act. When the duty on stamps was first proposed, the Americans made as little objection to it, as could be supposed to be made to any new tax whatever, Nay, several of their popular Orators and Leaders used considerable interest to be employed as Agents in the distribution of these stamps: and one among the rest, whom I need not name, was more than ordinary assidious in his application on this head: So that had the Act passed within the usual time, instead of being a flaming American Patriot, he would probably have acted the part of a Tax-Gatherer and an American Publican. But when the outs and the pouters on this side the water, saw the advantage which the Minister gave them by a whole year's delay, they eagerly seized the opportunity; Emissaries and Agents were dispatched into all quarters;—the Newspapers were filled with invectives against the new-intended Tax. It was injudicious!—it was ill-timed!—oppressive!—tyrannical!—and every thing

thing that was bad! letters upon letters were wrote to America to excite the People to affociate, to remonftrate, and even to revolt. The moft ample promifes were made from hence, of giving them all the affiftance which faction, and clamour, and mock-patriotifm, could mufter up. And then it was that this very man, this felf-intended Publican, changed fides, and commenced a zealous Patriot: Then he appeared at the Bar of the Houfe of Commons to cry down that very meafure which he himfelf had efpoufed; and then, as the avenging Angel of America,

" He rode in the Whirlwind to direct the Storm."

Well, the ftorm fell on the Minifter for the time being, and overfet him. Our Outs at Home became the Ins; and the ftorm having now done its bufinefs, they had no further occafion for it, were its moft obedient humble Servants, and wifhed it to fubfide. But here they found themfelves egregioufly miftaken. For the Americans had, in their turn, learnt the art of making tools of them, inftead of being made tools by them: fo that having been taught by thefe Preceptors to feel their own weight and independance, they were not to be wheedled by foothing and cajoling letters to give over their enterprize, or to become a tractable, obedient People for the future. In fhort, hence it came to pafs, that even during the continuance of this new and favourite adminiftration, the American fpirit was rifing all the while, inftead of sinking. And as like causes will always produce like effects, especially since things have been suffered to grow to such an height, evident it is to common sense, that any future attempt of the British Parliament to levy a tax on America, will meet with no better a fate than the Stamp Act has done. Moreover a years delay in laying it on will be just so much time given the Colonies to prepare for battle; and woe to that administration which shall propose it; for they will certainly be overturned by the same arts and managements which the former were, and with much greater ease.

I should now have done with this Gentleman's scheme, were it not that I find him, at page 28, making a kind of apology to the Americans for the conduct of our parliament in paying the King's debts of his civil list. And I own myself more hurt by this paragraph, than by all the rest of his pamphlet: for as I am thoroughly persuaded, he wrote from conviction, and not from any sinister views, one is sorry to find so able, so honest, and upright a man, carried away by the torrent of the times to such a degree, as to adopt notions, which are almost too crude for a club of Livery Politicians met in some blind alley at a city alehouse. His words are these:—" It is certain,
" that no such (exorbitant) grants as are above
" mentioned have been made, unless in the single
" instance of the sum of 513 000l. granted to
" his present Majesty for the discharge of the
" debts of his civil list. And in this case I
" can

"can easily suppose, that a motive of com-
"passion for a number of innocent persons
"who would otherwise have been sufferers from
"that load upon his Majesty's revenue, and
"an affectionate desire of relieving their ex-
"cellent Sovereign (who has in no instance en-
"deavoured to violate the liberties of his Sub-
"jects) from the unworthy streights and in-
"conveniences, ill becoming the royal dignity,
"into which some of his ministers had brought
"him by the injudicious management of his re-
"venue, may have induced many members of
"the House of Commons to consent to this
"grant, without any view to their own private
"interest; though at the same time I ac-
"knowledge it to be, considering all its cir-
"cumstances, a dangerous compliance, and
"not worthy to be drawn into example."

Now if the compliance of the Parliament in discharging this debt was dangerous, the reason must be, because the circumstance of contracting the debt itself was really infamous; therefore ought not to be avowed, but had better be suppressed in tenderness to the royal cause. But can this author point out any such infamous circumstances, if he were minded to make the discovery?—I dare answer for him, that he cannot. And as I will not suppose that he has more tales to tell than any other private Gentleman, or much less than he himself was an accomplice in, or privy to any such scenes of iniquity as are here insinuated.—I will now undertake to prove to him and the World, how

as

as great a debt as this, nay a much greater, might have been contracted in the space of ten years, without the least impeachment of waste, profusion, mismanagement, or any other misapplication whatsoever.

Every office, dignity, rank, or station has a certain character to sustain, which necessarily requires a correspondent train of expences; so that whether you consider the demands upon a King with a salary of 800,000l. a year, or the demands on a private Gentleman with only a clear rental of 800l. a year, the scale of expences must be proportionate, the demands and expences being relative one to the other.

We will therefore reason on what we are most conversant with, (and with respect to which we may be allowed to be competent judges) viz. on the case of a young Gentleman of a respectable ancient family, just come to take possesion of an Estate, which clears him 800l. a year.

1st. Therefore, being appointed Sheriff of the County, he must and ought to go through that expensive office in such manner as would reflect no disgrace on himself, or the respectable family from which he is descended (and the office of Sheriff belonging to a private Gentleman is of much the same import in point of expence, as the circumstances of a coronation in respect to Majesty.)

2dly. Many deaths and funerals within the above mentioned period create another article of expence, which must be borne; with this peculiar circumstance attending it, that tho' he must

must bury a grandfather suitably to his rank, also an uncle, aunts, a brother and sisters,—yet he himself acquires no addition of fortune by their deceases.

3dly. Several marriages in the family, and his own * in particular, bring on a third charge, which surely in reason and conscience ought not to be objected to.

4thly. Six or seven Christenings and lyings-in, expensive articles in all families, necessarily happen from the circumstance of the case to be peculiarly expensive in this: and yet neither the young Gentleman himself, nor any of his friends and well-wishers to the family, ought to have been supposed to have wished to have saved these extraordinary charges.

5thly. A train of unexpected visitants bring on another heavy load; and though they were not invited, yet, as they chose to come, they must be received with an hospitality suitable to his

---

* Some shrewd Politicians have been wise enough to ask, why did not his Majesty marry a large fortune, in order to reimburse some of these expences?—What large fortune would these Wiseacres have wished him to have married? A Dutchy or Principality on the Continent, in order to engage us still more in Continental measures?—Or was it to be a large landed Estate at home, to be annexed to the Crown, like another Dutchy of Lancaster?—This would have a fine influence on Electioneering, and English liberties.---But perhaps they meant, that he should have gone into the City, and have paid his addresses to Miss PLUMBE, the rich Grocer's daughter, or to Miss RESCOUNTERS the heiress of the great Broker in Change-Alley. And to be sure, such a match as this would have corresponded rarely well with the sublime ideas of City-politics. Our antient Nobility would have been delighted in giving the precedency to such illustrious Princes of the blood.

his and their dignity, and the relation of friendſhip and family-ties, ſubſiſting between them.

Add to this, 6thly, the uncommon dearneſs of all ſorts of proviſions, which for ſome years paſt hath exceeded any thing known in former times; and which alone hath actually ſwelled the amount of Houſe-keeping in every family to a very conſiderable ſum.

Now the young Gentleman having ſupported himſelf under theſe ſeveral preſſures and growing expences for ten years together, at laſt is obliged to requeſt his neareſt friends and deareſt relations to grant him ſome aſſiſtance; becauſe he is 513l. Or almoſt three quarters of a year in debt. Heavens! what a ſum! and is this all againſt which ſuch loud outcries have been raiſed? yes this is all! Indignant reader, whoever thou art, Engliſhman or American, lay thy hand on thy heart, and aſk thyſelf this plain queſtion, what wouldſt thou have thought of ſuch a young Man, had he been thine own Son, thy Grandſon, or the heir-apparent of thy fortune? And what ſort of treatment would he have deſerved at thy hands? Therefore, *mutato nomine* —But I will add no more: Let Nature and humanity, juſtice and equity, plead their own cauſe.

We have now, I think, very ſufficiently diſcuſſed every part of this gentleman's plan: nay, we have amply and particularly ſhewn, that his apology to the Americans in behalf of the Britiſh Parliament, for paying the arrears of his Majeſty's Civil Liſt, was quite a needleſs thing. For if no stronger proofs can be brought of their venality and corruption than this instance, they still may be safely trusted with the guardianship of those liberties and properties, which they have hitherto not only preserved, but also strengthened and encreased to a degree unknown before in this, or any other country. In one word the scheme of an union under our present consideration, is of such a nature, as would necessarily tend to exasperate both parties, instead of mollifying or reconciling either; and as the Americans have already given us to understand, both in their Provincial Assemblies, and at their General Congresses, that they will not accept of an union with us; and as Great-Britain ought not to petition for it; surely more need not be added for laying the scheme aside. Indeed the Gentleman himself, towards the close of his pamphlet, expresses but little hopes of its success: for, after all, the best use he can put it to, seems to be the justification of the Mother-Country in declaring war against the Colonies, in order to oblige them to submit to her authority, and to return to their obedience. So that this scheme of pacification is to end in a war at last. Therefore we are now come to consider the

THIRD PLAN.

The expediency of having recourse to arms, in order to compel the Colonies to submit to the authority and jurisdiction of the supreme council

council of the British Empire, the Parliament of GREAT-BRITAIN.

In regard to which important point, the gentleman reasons after the following manner : — "after such an offer (of an union, as above "described) and the contemptuous refusal of "it by the Colonies, we may well suppose, that "they (the inhabitants of Great-Britain) will "act as one man, to support the just and law- "ful, and necessary authority of the supreme "Legislature of the British Nation over all the "Dominions of the Crown. The justice of their "cause will give vigour to their measures ; and "the Colonies that shall have the folly and pre- "sumption to resist them, will be quickly re- "duced to obedience."

It is possible, nay indeed it is very probable, that if a war was to be speedily undertaken before Great-Britain and Ireland had been too much exhausted of their inhabitants, emigrating to North-America,—the forces of the Mother-Country might prevail, and America, however unwilling, be forced to submit. But alas! victory alone is but a poor compensation for all the blood and treasure which must be spilt on such an occasion. Not to mention, that after a conquest of their country, the Americans would certainly be less disposed, even than they are at present, to become our good customers, and to take our manufactures in return for those injuries and oppressions which they had suffered from us :—I say, injuries and oppressions ; because the Colonies would most undoubtedly
give

give no softer an appellation to this Conquest, tho' perhaps it would be no other in itself, than a just chastisement for the manifold offences they had committed. Moreover, as the Americans are endeavouring even at present to set up all sorts of mechanic trades in order to rival us, or at least to supersede the use of our manufactures in their country,---can any man suppose, that their ardor for setting up manufactures would be abated, by their being forced to deal at the one only European shop, which they most detested?

But what is still worse, if possible,---though the British troops might over-run the great Continent of North-America at first, it doth by no means follow, that they could be able to maintain a superiority in it afterwards for any length of time; and my reason is, because the governing of a country after a peace, is a much more arduous task, in certain circumstances, than the conquering it during a war. Thus for example, when a peace ensues (and surely it is not intended that we shall be forever in a state of war) then a civil constitution of some kind or other must necessarily be established; and in the case before us, there seems to be no other alternative, but either the permitting the Colonies to enjoy once more those advantages of English Liberty, and of an English Constitution, which they had forfeited; or else a resolution to govern them for the future by arbitrary sway and despotic power.

If the latter should be the plan adopted, I then humbly submit it to be duly weighed and considered, what a baneful influence this Government a la pruffe, would have on every other part of the British Empire. England free, and America in chains! And how soon would the enslaved part of the Constitution, and perhaps the greater, contaminate the free and the lesser? Nay, as America was found to increase in strength and numbers, an army of English-born soldiers (for no others could be trusted) first of 50,000, and afterwards perhaps of 100,000, would scarcely be sufficient to keep these turbulent spirits in awe, and to prevent them, at such a prodigious distance from the center of Government, from breaking out into insurrections and rebellions at every favourable opportunity. But if the former were to prevail, and a return of English Liberties was again to take place, it must also follow, that the system of trials by juries must return with them: and then, when America shall grow stronger and stronger every day, and England proportionably weaker, how is an insurrection to be quelled in America? and what English officer, civil or military, would dare to do it? Nay, I ask further, granting that he was so brave, or rather so fool-hardy, as to attempt to do his duty, who is to protect him in the execution of his office? Or how is he to be preserved, by due forms of law, against the determination of an American jury? a tumult is excited;———the military is called forth:

forth;—the soldiers are insulted;—many perhaps wounded, and some even killed. The patience of the officers worn out, and in their own defence, they are obliged to give the word of command to fire. The relations of those who fell by this fire, bring on an appeal of blood. The American jury find the officers who commanded, and perhaps the whole corps who fired, guilty of wilful murder; and then all the power of the Crown, legally exerted, is not able to save the lives of these poor innocent men. Pitiable sure is such a case; and yet it is a case which would and must frequently then happen in the natural course of things, according to our legal constitution.

Perhaps it might be said, that American juries are as conscientious as other juries in bringing in their verdicts according to law; and that it is very uncharitable even to suppose the contrary.—Be it so: But the question here turns on, What will be the suggestion of conscience in the breast of an American on such an occasion?—What would be his ideas of law, justice, or equity, when England and America stood in competition?—certainly, if ever the inhabitants of that country should come (and they are almost come already) to be fully persuaded that the British parliament hath no right to make laws either to tax or to govern them (and the having once beaten them will not be taken as a convincing proof that we always have either the right or the power to beat them) then every attempt towards throwing

throwing off this odious yoke, would appear in their eye, as so many noble struggles for the cause of liberty: and therefore the base English hireling, who would dare to injure this sacred cause, deserved to die a thousand deaths. Such undoubtedly would be the language, and such the sentiments of the great majority of Americans whenever such a case should happen. In a word, an erroneous conscience, and a false zeal, would have just the same bad effects in the new world respecting civil government, as they formerly had in the old, in regard to religion: And therefore, either way, whether we should treat these Americans as an enslaved people, or whether we should restore to them, after a conquest, the same constitution which we enjoy ourselves, the final event would come to this,—That England would be the greatest sufferer; and that America is not to be governed against its own inclinations. Wherefore let us now now come to the

FOURTH PLAN,

Viz. To consent that America should become the general seat of Empire, and that GREAT BRITAIN and IRELAND, should be governed by Vice-Roys sent over from the Court Residencies either at Philadelphia, or New-York, or at some other American Imperial, City.

Now, wild as such a scheme may appear, there are certainly some Americans who seriously embrace it: and the late prodigious swarms of Emigrants encourage them to suppose, that a time is approaching, when the Seat of Empire

pire muſt be changed. But whatever events may be in the womb of time, or whatever revolutions may happen in the riſe and fall of Empires, there is not the leaſt probability, that this country ſhould ever become a province to North-America. For granting even, that it would be ſo weakened and enfeebled by theſe Colony-drains, as not to be able to defend itſelf from invaders, yet America is at too great a diſtance to invade it at firſt, much leſs to defend the conqueſt of it afterwards, againſt the neighbouring powers of Europe: and as to any notion that we ourſelves ſhould prefer an American yoke to any other,—this ſuppoſition is chimerical indeed; becauſe it is much more probable, were things to come to ſuch a dreadful criſis, that the Engliſh would rather ſubmit to a French yoke, than to an American; as being the leſſer indignity of the two. So that in ſhort, if we muſt reaſon in politics according to the Newtonian Principles in Philoſophy. The idea of the leſſer country gravitating towards the greater, muſt lead us to conclude, that this Iſland would rather gravitate towards the Continent of Europe, than towards the Continent of America; unleſs indeed we ſhould add one extravagance to another, by ſuppoſing that the Americans are to conquer all the world; and in that caſe I do allow, that England muſt become a Province to America. But

We come now to conſider the

FIFTH PLAN. Viz.

To propoſe to ſeparate entirely from the
North-

North-American-Colonies, by declaring them to be a free and independent people, over whom we lay no claim; and then by offering to guarantee this freedom and independence against all foreign invaders whatever.

And, in fact, what is all this but the natural and even the neceſſary corollary to be deduced from each of the former reaſons and obſervations? For if we neither can govern the Americans, nor be governed by them; if we can neither unite with them, nor ought to ſubdue them;—what remains, but to part with them on as friendly terms as we can? and if any man ſhould think that he can reaſon better from the above premiſes, let him try.

But as the idea of ſeparation, and the giving up the Colonies forever will ſhock many weak people, who think, that there is neither happineſs nor ſecurity but in an overgrown unwieldy Empire, I will for their ſakes enter into a diſcuſſion of the ſuppoſed diſadvantages attending ſuch a disjunction; and then ſhall ſet forth the manifold advantages.

The firſt and capital ſuppoſed diſadvantage is, That if we ſeparate from the Colonies, we ſhall loſe their trade. But why ſo? and how does this appear? The Colonies, we know by experience, will trade with any people, even with their bittereſt enemies, during the hotteſt of a war, and a war undertaken at their own earneſt requeſt, and for their own ſakes;—the Colonies, I ſay, will trade even with them, provided they ſhall find it their intereſt ſo to do. Why then ſhould

should any man suppose, that the same self-interest will not induce them to trade with us? with us, I say, who are to commit no hostilities against them, but on the contrary, are still to remain, if they please, their Guardians and Protectors?

Granting, therefore, that NORTH-AMERICA was to become independent of us, and we of them, the question now before us will turn on this single point,—can the Colonists, in a general way, trade with any other European State to greater advantage than they can with Great-Britain? If they can, they certainly will; but if they cannot, we shall still retain their custom, notwithstanding we have parted with every claim of authority and jurisdiction over them. Now, the native commodities and merchandize of North-America, which are the most saleable at an European market, are chiefly lumber, Ships, iron, train-oil, flax-seed, skins, furs, pitch, tar, turpentine, pearl-ashes, indigo, tobacco, and rice: and I do aver, that, excepting rice and tobacco, there is hardly one of these articles, for which an American could get so good a price any where else, as he can in Great-Britain and Ireland. Nay, I ought to have excepted only rice; for as to tobacco, tho' great quantities of it are re-exported into France, yet it is well known, that the French might raise it at home, if they would, much cheaper than they can import it from our Colonies. The fact is this,—The Farm of tobacco is one of the great five farms, which make up the chief part of the Royal revenue; and therefore the Farmers General, for bye-ends of their own, have hitherto had interest enough with the Court to prohibit the cultivation of it in Old France, under the severest penalties. But nevertheless the real French Patriots, and particularly the Marquis de Mirabeau, have fully demonstrated, that it is the interest of the French government to encourage the cultivation of it; and have pointed out a sure and easy method of collecting the duties; which was the sole pretence of the Farmers General for soliciting a prohibition. So that it is apprehended, that the French government will at last open their eyes in this respect, and allow the cultivation of it. Tobacco therefore being likely to be soon out of the question, the only remaining article is rice; and this, it must be acknowledged, would bear a better price at the Hamburgh or Dutch markets than it generally doth in England. But as this is only one article, out of many, it should be further considered, that even the Ships which import rice into England, generally bring such other produce as would not be saleable to advantage in other parts of Europe: so that there is no great cause to fear, that we should considerably lose the trade even of this article, were the Colonies to be dismembered from us. Not to mention that all the coasts of the Mediterranean and the south of Europe are already supplied with rice from the Colonies, in the same manner

ner as if there had been an actual separation; ——no rice-ship bound to any place south of Cape Finisterre being at all obliged to touch at any Port of Great-Britain. So much, therefore, as to the staple exports of the Colonies.

Let us now consider their IMPORTS. And here one thing is very clear and certain, that whatever goods, merchandize, or manufactures, the merchants of Great-Britain can sell to the rest of Europe, they might sell the same to the Colonies, if wanted: Because it is evident, that the Colonies could not purchase such goods at a cheaper rate at any other European market. Now, let any one cast his eye over the bills of exports from London, Bristol, Liverpool, Hull, Glasgow, &c. &c. and then he will soon discover that excepting gold and silver lace, wines and brandies, some sorts of silks and linens, and perhaps a little paper and Gun-powder; I say, excepting these few articles, Great-Britain is become a kind of a general mart for most other commodities: and indeed were it not so, how is it conceivable, that so little a spot as this island could have made such a figure either in peace or war, as it hath lately done? How is it possible that after having contracted a debt of nearly one hundred and forty millions, we should nevertheless be able to make more rapid progresses in all sorts of improvements, useful and ornamental, public and private, agricolic and commercial, than any other nation ever did?---Fact it is, that

these

these improvements have been made of late years, and are daily making: and facts are stubborn things.

But, says the objector, you allow, that gold and silver lace,---that wines and brandies, some sorts of silks,———some sorts of paper, gun-powder, and perhaps other articles, can be purchased at certain European markets on cheaper terms than they can in England: and therefore it follows, that we should certainly lose these branches of commerce by a separation, even supposing that we could retain the rest. Indeed even this doth not follow; because we have lost them already, as far as it was the interest of the colonies, that we should lose them. And if any man can doubt of this, let him but consider, that the lumber, and provision-vessels, which are continually running down from Boston, Rhode-Island, New-York, Philadelphia, Charles-Town, &c. &c. to Martinico, and the other French islands, bring home in return not only sugars and molasses, but also French wines, silks, gold and silver lace, and in short every other article, in which they can find a profitable account: Moreover those ships, which sail to Eustatia and Curacoa, trade with the Dutch, and consequently with all the North of Europe, on the same principle. And as the ships which steer south of Cape Finisterre, what do they do?—Doubtless, they purchase whatever commodities they find it their interest to purchase, and carry them home to North-America. Indeed what would hinder them from acting

acting agreeably to their own ideas of advantage in these respects? The Custom-House Officers, perhaps, you may say, will hinder them. But alas! the Custom-House Officers of North-America, if they were ten times more numerous, and ten times more uncorrupt than they are, could not possibly guard a tenth part of the coast. In short these things are so very notorious that they cannot be disputed; and therefore, were the whole trade of North-America to be divided into two branches, viz. the voluntary, resulting from a free choice of the Americans themselves, pursuing their own interest, and the involuntary, in consequence of compulsory Acts of the British Parliament;—this latter would appear so very small and inconsiderable, as hardly to deserve a name in an estimate of national commerce.

The 2d objection against giving up the Colonies is, that such a measure would greatly decrease our shipping and navigation, and consequently diminish the breed of sailors. But this objection has been fully obviated already: For if we shall not lose our trade, at least in any important degree, even with the northern Colonies (and most probably we shall encrease it with other countries) then it follows, that neither the quantity of shipping, nor the breed of sailors, can suffer any considerable diminution: So that this supposition is merely a panic, and has no foundation. Not to mention, that in proportion as the Americans shall be obliged to exert themselves to defend their

own

own coasts, in case of a war; in the same proportion shall Great-Britain be exonorated from that burden, and shall have more ships and men at command to protect her own channel Trade, and for other services.

The 3d objection is, That if we were to give up these Colonies, the French would take immediate possession of them. Now this objection is intirely built on the following very wild, very extravagant, and absurd suppositions.

1st, It supposes, that the Colonists themselves, who cannot brook our government, would like a French one much better. Great-Britain, it seems, doth not grant them liberty enough; and therefore they have recourse to France to obtain more:—That is, in plain English, our mild and limited Government, where prerogative is ascertained by law, where every man is at liberty to seek for redress, and where popular clamours too often carry every thing before them,—is nevertheless too severe, too oppressive, and too tyrannical for the spirits and genius of Americans to bear; and therefore they will apply to an arbitrary, despotic Government, where the people have no share in the Legislature, where there is no liberty of the Press and where General Warrants and Lettres des Cachets are irresistible, in order to enjoy greater freedoms than they have at present, and to be rescued from the intolerable yoke, under which they now groan. What monstrous absurdities are these? But even this is not all: For these Americans are represented by this supposition,

as

as not only preferring a French government to a British, but even to a government of their own modelling and chusing! For after they are set free from any submission to their Mother-Country; after they are told, that for the future they must endeavour to please themselves, seeing we cannot please them; then, instead of attempting to frame any popular governments for redressing those evils, of which they now so bitterly complain,—they are represented as throwing themselves at once into the arms of France;—the Republican spirit is to subside; the doctrine of passive obedience and non-resistance is to succeed; and, instead of setting up for freedom and independence, they are to glory in having the honour of being numbered among the slaves of the Grand Monarch!

But 2dly, this matter may be further considered in another point of view: for if it should be said, that the Americans might still retain their Republican spirit, tho' they submitted to a French government, because the French, through policy, would permit them so to do; then it remains to be considered, whether any arbitrary government can dispense with such liberties as a Republican spirit will require. An absolute freedom of the Press! No controul on the liberty either of speaking or writing on matters of state! Newspapers and Pamphlets filled with the bitterest invectives against the measures of government! Associations formed in every quarter to cry down Ministerial Hirelings, and their dependants!

The

The votes and refolutions of the Provincial Affemblies to affert their own authority and independence! No landing of troops from Old France to quell Infurrections! No raifing of new levies in America! No quartering of Troops! No building of forts, or erecting of garrifons! And, to fum up all, no raifing of money without the exprefs confent and approbation of the Provincial American Parliaments firft obtained for each of thefe purpofes! Now I afk any reafonable man whether thefe things are compatible with any idea of an arbitrary, defpotic government? Nay more, whether the French King himfelf, or his minifters would wifh to have fuch notions as thefe inftilled into the fubjects of Old France? Yet inftilled they muft be while a communication is kept open between the two Countries; while correfpondences are carried on; letters, pamphlets, and newfpapers, pafs and re-pafs; and in fhort while the Americans are permitted to come into France, and Frenchmen into America. So much therefore as to this clafs of objections. Indeed I might have infifted further, that Great Britain alone could at any time prevent fuch an acquifition to be made by France, as is here fuppofed, if fhe fhould think it neceffary to interfere, and if fuch an acquifition of territory would really and truly be an addition of ftrength in the political balance and fcale of power. But furely I have faid enough; and therefore let us now haften briefly to point out,

The

The manifold Advantages attendant on such a Plan.

And 1st, A disjunction from the nothern Colonies would effectually put a stop to our present emigrations. By the laws of the land it is made a capital offence to inveigle artificers and mechanics to leave the kingdom, but this law is unhappily superseded at present as far as the Colonies are concerned. Therefore when they come to be dismembered from us, it will operate as strongly against them, and their kidnappers, as against others, and here it may be worth while to observe, that the emigrants, who lately sailed in such multitudes from the North of Scotland and more especially from the North of Ireland, were far from being the most indigent, or the least capable of subsisting in their own Country. No; it was not poverty or necessity which compelled, but ambition which enticed them to forsake their native soil. For after they began to taste the sweets of industry, and to partake of the comforts of life, then they became a valuable prey for these harpies. In short, such were the persons to whom these seducers principally applied; because they found that they had gotten some little substance together worth devouring. They therefore told them many plausible stories--- that if they would emigrate to North-America, they might have estates for nothing and become gentlemen forever; whereas, if they remained at home, they had nothing to expect beyond the Condition of a wretched Journeyman, or a small laborious farmer. Nay, one of these false guides was known to have put out public advertisements, some few years ago in the North of Ireland, wherein he engaged to carry all, who would follow him, into such a glorious Country, where there was neither tax, nor tythe, nor Landlord's rent to be paid. This was enough: it took with thousands: and this he might safely engage to do. But at the same time, he ought to have told them (as Bishop BERKLEY in his queries justly observes) That a man may possess twenty miles square in this Country, and yet not be able to get a dinner.

2dly. Another great advantage to be derived from a separation is, that we shall then save between 3 and 400,000l. a year, by being discharged from the payment of any civil or military establishment belonging to the Colonies; for which generous benefaction we receive at present no other return than invectives and reproaches.

3dly. The ceasing of the payment of bounties on certain Colony productions will be another great saving; perhaps not less than 200,000l. a year: and it is very remarkable, that the goods imported from the Colonies in consequence of these bounties, could not have been imported into any other part of Europe, were there a liberty to do it; because the freight and first cost would have amounted to more than they could be sold for: so that in fact we give premiums to the Colonies for selling goods to us, which would not have been sold at all any where else. However, when the present bounties shall cease, we may then consider, at our leisure,

leisure, whether it would be right to give them again, or not; and we shall have it in our power to favour that country most which will shew the greatest favour to us, and to our manufactures.

4thly, When we are no longer connected with the Colonies by the imaginary tie of an identity of government, than our merchant-exporters and manufacturers will have a better chance of having their debts paid, than they have at present: For as matters now stand, the Colonists chuse to carry their ready cash to other nations, while they are contracting debts with their Mother-Country, with whom they think they can take great liberties: and provided they are trusted, they care not to what amount this debt shall rise :—For when the time for payment draws on, they are seized with a fit of patriotism; and then confederacies and associations are to discharge all arrears; or at least, are to postpone the payment of them SINE DIE.

5thly, After a separation from the Colonies, our influence over them will be much greater than ever it was, since they began to feel their own weight and importance: For at present we are looked upon in no better a light than that of robbers and usurpers; whereas, we shall then be considered as their protectors, mediators, and benefactors. The moment a separation takes effect, intestine quarrels will begin: For it is well known, that the seeds of discord and dissention between Province and Province are now ready to shoot forth; and that they are only kept down by the present combination
of

all the Colonies against us, whom they unhappily fancy to be their common enemy. When therefore this object of their hatred shall be removed by a declaration on our parts, that, so far from usurping all authority, we, from henceforward will assume none at all against their own consent; the weaker Provinces will intreat our protection against the stronger; and the less cautious against the more crafty and designing: So that in short, in proportion as their republican spirit shall intrigue and cabal, they will split into parties, divide and sub-divide, in the same proportion shall we be called in to become their general Umpires and Referees. Not to mention, that many of the late and present Emigrants, when they shall see these storms arising all around them, and when their promised earthly paradise turns out to be a dreary, unwholesome, inhospitable, and howling wilderness, many of them, I say, will probably return to us again, and take refuge at last in Old England, with all its faults and imperfections.

Lastly, Our WEST-INDIA Islands themselves will receive signal benefit by this separation. Indeed their size and situation render them incapable of subtracting all obedience from us; and yet the bad precedents of their neighbours on the Continent hath sometimes prompted them to shew as refractory a spirit as they well could.

But when they come to perceive, what are the bitter effects of this untractable disposition, exemplified in the case of the NORTH-AMERICANS, it is probable, it is reasonable to conclude, that they will learn wisdom by the miscarriages

carriages and sufferings of these unhappy people; and that from henceforward they will revere the authority of a Government, which has the fewest faults, and grants the greatest liberty, of any yet known upon earth.

But after all, there is one thing more, to which I must make some reply. Many, perhaps most of my readers, will be apt to ask, what is all this about? And what doth this Author really mean? Can he seriously think, that because he hath taken such pains to prove a separation to be a right measure, that therefore we shall separate in good earnest? and is he still so much a novice as not to know, that measures are rarely adopted merely because they are right, but because they can serve a present turn? Therefore let it be asked, what present convenience or advantage doth he propose either to administration, or to anti-administration, by the execution of his plan? This is coming to the point, and without it, all that he has said will pass for nothing.

I frankly acknowledge, I propose no present convenience or advantage to either; nay, I firmly believe, that no Minister, as things are now circumstanced, will dare to do so much good to his Country; and as to the Herd of Anti-Ministers, they, I am persuaded, would not wish to see it done; because it would deprive them of one of their most plentiful sources for clamour and detraction: and yet I have observed, and have myself had some experience, that measures evidently right will prevail at last: Therefore I make not the least doubt but that a separation
from

from the northern Colonies, and also another right measure, viz. a complete union and incorporation with Ireland (however unpopular either of them may now appear) will both take place within half a century: And perhaps that which happens to be first accomplished, will greatly accelerate the accomplishment of the other. Indeed almost all people are apt to startle at first at bold truths: But it is observable, that in proportion as they grow familiarized to them, and can see and consider them from different points of view, their fears subside, and they become reconciled by degrees: Nay, it is not an uncommon thing for them to adopt those salutary measures afterwards with as much zeal and ardor as they had rejected them before with anger and indignation.

Need I add, that the man, who will have resolution enough to advance any bold unwelcome truth (unwelcome I mean at its first appearance) ought to be such an one, whose competency of fortune, joined to a natural independency of spirit, places him in that happy situation, as to be equally indifferent to the smiles, or frowns either of the great, or the vulgar;

Lastly, some persons perhaps may wonder, that, being myself a clergyman, I have said nothing about the persecution which the Church of England daily suffers in America, by being denied those rights which every other sect of Christians so amply enjoys. I own I have hitherto omitted to make mention of that circumstance, not thro' inadvertance, but by design; as being unwilling to embarrass my general plan with what

might

might be deemed by some readers to be foreign to the subject: and therefore I shall be very short in what I have to add at present.

That each religious persuasion ought to have a full toleration from the state to worship Almighty God, according to the dictates of their own consciences, is to me so clear a case, that I shall not attempt to make it clearer; and nothing but the maintaining some monstrous opinion inconsistent with the safety of society,—— and that not barely in theory and speculation, but by open practice and outward actions,——I say, nothing but the avowedly maintaining of such dangerous principles can justify the magistrate in abridging any set of men of these their natural rights. It is also equally evident, that the church of England doth not, cannot fall under the censure of holding opinions inconsistent with the safety of the state, and the good of mankind,———even her enemies themselves being judges: and yet the church of England alone doth not enjoy a toleration in that full extent, which is granted to the members of every other denomination. What then can be the cause of putting so injurious a distinction between the church of England, and other churches in this respect? the reason is plain. The Americans have taken it into their heads to believe, that an episcopate would operate as some further tie upon them, not to break loose from those obligations which they owe to the Mother-Country; and that this is to be used as an engine, under the masque of religion, to rivet those chains, which they imagine we are
forging

forging for them. Let therefore the Mother-Country herself resign up all claim of authority over them, as well ecclesiastical as civil; let her declare North America to be independent of Great-Britain in every respect whatever;--- let her do this, I say, and then all their fears will vanish away, and their panics be at an end: And then a bishop, who has no more connections with England either in church or state, than he has with Germany, Sweden, or any other country, will be no longer looked upon in America as a monster, but a man. In short, when all motives for opposition will be at an end, it is observable, that the opposition itself soon ceases and dies away. In a word an episcopate may then take place; and whether this new Ecclesiastical officer be called from a name derived from the Greek, the Latin, or the German,---that is, whether he be stiled episcopus, superintendent, supervisor, overseer, &c. &c. it matters not, provided he be invested with competent authority to ordain and confirm such of the members of his own persuasion, as shall voluntarily offer themselves, and to inspect the lives and morals of his own clergy.

F I N I S.

A few more WORDS, on the FREEDOM of the PRESS, Addressed by the PRINTER, to the FRIENDS of LIBERTY in AMERICA.

Since the PRESS is FREE, LONG may it REMAIN FREE.
BELL.

IT was the saying of an Ancient, and wise ENGLISHMAN, (TINDAL), who lived at the time of the Glorious Revolution in 1688, That, "While the Freedom of the "PRESS is preserved, all other Liberties, "both Civil and Religious, will be secured to "us, under so faithful a Guardian." And it is the declaration of the modern, and noble VIRGINIANS, "that the Freedom of the "PRESS is one of the great bulwarks of "Liberty, and can never be restrained but by "despotic governments." Notwithstanding these worthy and estimable authorities, if there are yet any number of mistaken men existing, who under the specious pretence of there being a necessity at some trying exigence for a temporary restriction of the FREEDOM of the PRESS, and their foolish advice should at any one time be adopted, we may then bid a final adieu to every thing pertaining to Liberty: For it is more than probable, that like unto the wretched British Parliament, in the Year 1716, who pretended, there were at that time, too many Jacobites in the nation, to suffer the triennial election of Members for that House.— They then tyrannically constituted themselves into a septennial parliament: And for the last sixty years, have illegally and au-
daciously

On the Freedom of the Press.

dauciously committed one continued insult upon the constitution of the Kingdom, and upon the understandings of the whole body of the people in Great Britain.—Now, if Americans will agreeable to the good old English advice—

"Learn to be wise, from others harm,
"Then, they shall do full well.

But, if according to the opinion of some violents against the freedom of enquiry, they will unwisely trample upon that greatest of all privileges, the Liberty of the PRESS; then will they, like the foolish people of Britain, commit suicide on their own liberties, and thus, entail upon themselves, the scorn and contempt of all true and consistent friends to real Liberty; because, if new modes of Government, are either in reality, or in appearance, approaching towards the inhabitants of America; it is more peculiarly necessary on these extraordinary occasions, that the Liberty of the PRESS should be freely exerted: For, if in these changes, we do not fully retain all our present happy privileges, but weakly suffer any restrictions or curtailings of Liberty to advance upon us with new establishments, it will afterwards be next to impossible, to regain the desirable possession.

Thus far, the Printer still thinks it indispensibly his duty to support the Freedom of the PRESS, in which all the lovers of genuine Liberty are deeply interested. And, if there are any, who think otherwise, they may if they please, peruse what follows. A

A SHORT ANSWER TO SOME CRITICISMS.

Which were Exhibited under the Signature of ARISTIDES: Containing, a reasonable Vindication of the Propriety of those Defences of the LIBERTY of the PRESS, Which were Annexed to PLAIN TRUTH, And to the Additions to PLAIN TRUTH; Published, in 1776. EXTRACTED from an Old Pamphlet, Published in the Year 1756, Entitled PLAIN TRUTH: Or, Serious Considerations on the Present State of the City of PHILADELPHIA, and Province of PENNSYLVANIA.

By a Tradesman of PHILADELPHIA.

"IT is said the wise Italians make this proverbial Remark on our Nation, viz The English FEEL, but they do not SEE. That is, they are sensible of inconveniencies when they are present, but do not take sufficient care to prevent them: Their natural courage makes them too little apprehensive of danger, so that they are often surprized by it, unprovided of the proper means of security. When 'tis too late they are sensible of their imprudence: After great fires, they provide
"buckets

On the Freedom of the Press.

"buckets and engines: After a pestilence they think of keeping clean their streets and common shores: and when a town has been sack'd by their enemies, they provide for its defence. This kind of AFTER-WISDOM is indeed so common with us, as to occasion the vulgar, tho' very significant saying, *When the Steed is stolen, it is time to shut the stable door.*"

(And the Printer of these useful and necessary DEFENCES, takes the liberty to insert here,)

After the freedom of the Press hath been circumscribed by the ignorance or malice of mistaken zealots, it will then be time to cringe to some cowardly Printer, to beg he would support its Liberty.

N. B. The *quibblings* of Aristides, concerning the *Words* first Edition, were sufficiently confuted five days before they made their appearance, by the publication of the second Edition of PLAIN TRUTH.

Now

RESEARCH LIBRARY OF COLONIAL AMERICANA

An Arno Press Collection

Histories

Acrelius, Israel. **A History of New Sweden; Or, The Settlements on the River Delaware** ... Translated with an Introduction and Notes by William M. Reynolds. Historical Society of Pennsylvania, MEMOIRS, XI, Philadelphia, 1874.

Belknap, Jeremy. **The History of New Hampshire.** 3 vols., Vol. 1—Philadelphia, 1784 (Reprinted Boston, 1792), Vol. 2—Boston, 1791, Vol. 3—Boston, 1792.

Browne, Patrick. **The Civil and Natural History of Jamaica. In Three Parts** ... London, 1756. Includes 1789 edition Linnaean index.

[Burke, Edmund]. **An Account of the European Settlements in America. In Six Parts** ... London, 1777. Two volumes in one.

Chalmers, George. **An Introduction to the History of the Revolt of the American Colonies:** Being a Comprehensive View of Its Origin, Derived From the State Papers Contained in the Public Offices of Great Britain. London, 1845. Two volumes in one.

Douglass, William. **A Summary, Historical and Political, of the First Planting, Progressive Improvements, and Present State of the British Settlements in North-America.** Boston, 1749–1752. Two volumes in one.

Edwards, Bryan. **The History, Civil and Commercial, of the British Colonies in the West Indies.** Dublin, 1793–1794. Two volumes in one.

Hughes, Griffith. **The Natural History of Barbados. In Ten Books.** London, 1750.

[Franklin, Benjamin]. **An Historical Review of the Constitution and Government of Pennsylvania, From Its Origin** . . . London, 1759.

Hubbard, William. **A General History of New England, From the Discovery to MDCLXXX.** (*In* Massachusetts Historical Society, COLLECTIONS, Series 2, vol. 5, 6, 1815. Reprinted 1848.)

Hutchinson, Thomas. **The History of the Colony of Massachusetts Bay** . . . 3 vols., Boston, 1764–1828.

Keith, Sir William. **The History of the British Plantations in America** . . . London, 1738.

Long, Edward. **The History of Jamaica:** Or, General Survey of the Antient and Modern State of that Island . . . 3 vols., London, 1774.

Mather, Cotton. **Magnalia Christi Americana;** Or, The Ecclesiastical History of New-England From . . . the Year 1620, Unto the Year . . . 1698. In Seven Books. London, 1702.

Mather, Increase. **A Relation of the Troubles Which Have Hapned in New-England, By Reason of the Indians There From the Year 1614 to the Year 1675** . . . Boston, 1677.

Smith, Samuel. **The History of the Colony of Nova-Caesaria, Or New-Jersey** . . . **to the Year 1721** . . . Burlington, N.J., 1765.

Thomas, Sir Dalby. **An Historical Account of the Rise and Growth of the West-India Collonies,** and of the Great Advantages They are to England, in Respect to Trade. London, 1690.

Trumbull, Benjamin. **A Complete History of Connecticut,** Civil and Ecclesiastical, From the Emigration of Its First Planters, From England, in the Year 1630, to the Year 1764; and to the Close of the Indian Wars . . . New Haven, 1818. Two volumes in one.

Personal Narratives and Promotional Literature

Byrd, William. **The Secret Diary of William Byrd of Westover, 1709–1712,** edited by Louis B. Wright and Marion Tinling. Richmond, Va., 1941.

Byrd, William. **The London Diary (1717–1721) and Other Writings,** edited by Louis B. Wright and Marion Tinling. New York, 1958.

A Genuine Narrative of the Intended Conspiracy of the Negroes at Antigua. Extracted From an Authentic Copy of a Report, Made to the Chief Governor of the Carabee Islands, by the Commissioners, or Judges Appointed to Try the Conspirators. Dublin, 1737.

Gookin, Daniel. **An Historical Account of the Doings and Sufferings of the Christian Indians in New England in the Years 1675, 1676, 1677** . . . (*In* American Antiquarian Society, Worcester, Mass. ARCHAEOLOGIA AMERICANA. TRANSACTIONS AND COLLECTIONS. Cambridge, 1836. vol. 2.)

Gookin, Daniel. **Historical Collections of the Indians in New England.** Of Their Several Nations, Numbers, Customs, Manners, Religion and Government, Before the English Planted There . . . Boston, 1792.

Morton, Thomas. **New English Canaan or New Canaan.** Containing an Abstract of New England, Composed in Three Books . . . Amsterdam, 1637.

Sewall, Samuel. **Diary of Samuel Sewall, 1674–1729.** (*In* Massachusetts Historical Society. COLLECTIONS, 5th Series, V–VII, 1878–1882.) Three volumes.

Virginia: Four Personal Narratives. (Hamor, Ralph. *A True Discourse on the Present Estate of Virginia . . . Till the 18 of June 1614* . . . London, 1615/Hariot, Thomas. *A Briefe and True Report of the New Found Land of Virginia* . . . London, 1588/Percy, George. *A Trewe Relacyon of the Proceedings and Ocurrentes of Momente Which Have Happened in Virginia From . . . 1609, Until . . . 1612.* (In *Tyler's Quarterly Historical and Genealogical Magazine,* Vol. III, 1922.)/Rolf, John. *Virginia in 1616.* (In *Virginia Historical Register and Literary Advertiser,* Vol. I, No. III, July, 1848.) New York, 1972.

Winthrop, John. **The History of New England From 1630–1649.** Edited by James Savage. Boston, 1825–1826. Two volumes in one.

New England Puritan Tracts of the Seventeenth Century

Cobbett, Thomas. **The Civil Magistrate's Power in Matters of Religion Modestly Debated** . . . London, 1653.

Cotton, John. **The Bloudy Tenent, Washed, and Made White in the Bloud of the Lambe** . . . London, 1647.

Cotton, John. **A Brief Exposition with Practical Observations Upon the Whole Book of Canticles.** London, 1655.

Cotton, John. **Christ the Fountaine of Life:** Or, Sundry Choyce Sermons on Part of the Fift Chapter of the First Epistle of St. John. London, 1651.

Cotton, John. **Two Sermons.** (*Gods Mercie Mixed with His Justice* . . . London, 1641/*The True Constitution of a Particular Visible Church, Proved by Scripture* . . . London, 1642.) New York, 1972.

Eliot, John. **The Christian Commonwealth:** Or, The Civil Policy of the Rising Kingdom of Jesus Christ. London, 1659.

Hooker, Thomas. **The Application of Redemption,** By the Effectual Work of the Word, and Spirit of Christ, for the Bringing Home of Lost Sinners to God. London, 1657.

H[ooker], T[homas]. **The Christian's Two Chiefe Lessons,** Viz. Selfe Deniall, and Selfe Tryall . . . London, 1640.

Hooker, Thomas. **A Survey of the Summe of Church-Discipline** Wherein the Way of the Churches of New England is Warranted Out of the Word, and All Exceptions of Weight, Which Are Made Against It, Answered . . . London, 1648.

Increase Mather Vs. Solomon Stoddard: Two Puritan Tracts. (Mather, Increase. *The Order of the Gospel, Professed and Practised by the Churches of Christ in New-England* . . . Boston, 1700/Stoddard, Solomon. *The Doctrine of Instituted Churches Explained, and Proved From the Word of God.* London, 1700.) New York, 1972.

Mather, Cotton. **Ratio Disciplinae Fratrum Nov-Anglorum.** A Faithful Account of the Discipline Professed and Practised, in the Churches of New England. Boston, 1726.

Mather, Richard. **Church Covenant:** Two Tracts. (*Church-Government and Church-Covenant Discussed, in an Answer to the Elders of the Severall Churches in New-England* . . . London, 1643/*An Apologie of the Churches in New-England for Church-Covenant, Or, A Discourse Touching the Covenant Between God and Men, and Especially Concerning Church-Covenant* . . . London, 1643.) New York, 1972.

The Imperial System

[Blenman, Jonathan]. **Remarks on Several Acts of Parliament Relating More Especially to the Colonies Abroad** . . . London, 1742.

British Imperialism: Three Documents. (Berkeley, George. *A Proposal for the Better Supplying of Churches in our Foreign Plantations, and for Converting the Savage Americans to Christianity by a College to be Erected in the Summer Islands, Otherwise Called the Isles of Bermuda . . .* London, 1724/[Fothergill, John]. *Considerations Relative to the North American Colonies.* London, 1765/*A Letter to a Member of Parliament Concerning the Naval-Store Bill . . .* London, 1720.) New York, 1972.

Coke, Roger. **A Discourse of Trade** . . . London, 1670.

[D'Avenant, Charles]. **An Essay Upon the Government of the English Plantations on the Continent of America** (1701). An Anonymous Virginian's Proposals for Liberty Under the British Crown, With Two Memoranda by William Byrd. Edited by Louis B. Wright. San Marino, Calif., 1945.

Dummer, Jeremiah. **A Defence of the New-England Charters** . . . London, 1721.

Gee, Joshua. **The Trade and Navigation of Great Britain Considered:** Shewing that Surest Way for a Nation to Increase in Riches, is to Prevent the Importation of Such Foreign Commodities as May Be Rais'd at Home. London, 1729.

[Little, Otis]. **The State of Trade in the Northern Colonies Considered;** With an Account of Their Produce, and a Particular Description of Nova Scotia . . . London, 1748.

Tucker, Jos[iah]. **The True Interest of Britain, Set Forth in Regard to the Colonies:** And the Only Means of Living in Peace and Harmony With Them, Including Five Different Plans for Effecting this Desirable Event . . . Philadelphia, 1776.

LIBRARY OF DAVIDSON COLLEGE

Books on regular loan may be checked out for two weeks. Books must be presented at the Circulation Desk in order to be renewed. A fine of five cents a day will be charged after date due. Special books are subject to special regulations at the discretion of library staff.